空手道
Karate Made Simple

4 Karate Origins and Expansion

Maiko Nakashima
with the Japan Karate Federation

The Oliver Press, Inc.
Minneapolis

INTRODUCTION

Karate-do is a Japanese *budo*, or martial art. It originated on the Japanese island of Okinawa and spread to the rest of Japan. *Budo* is a part of Japanese culture that is based on traditional combat skills. Like all forms of martial arts, the goal of karate is not just to defeat your opponent; it is also to discipline heart, mind, and body through practice and respect for one's opponents.

Karate-do, or the "way of karate," is now known around the world as "karate." In 2010, the World Karate Federation (WKF) had members in 187 countries, and estimates that around 50 million people study karate. Every two years, there is an international tournament, the World Karate Championships, in which athletes gather from all over the world to compete.

By reading this book, you will be able to answer these questions:

- **What law led to the development of karate?**
- **How did World War II influence the expansion of karate?**

Recently, there has been a movement in Japan to place more importance on traditional Japanese culture, including karate. Starting in 2012, all middle-school students were required to take a *budo* class. Imagine being required to take karate as a gym class!

This series is divided into four books that will introduce you to what you need to know to master karate in an easy-to-understand way.

In this series, you will learn how this martial art spread from a small island to become a worldwide phenomenon.

CONTENTS

The Beginnings of Karate

Karate developed from the ancient martial arts of Okinawa. Let's look at how karate expanded from this small Japanese island.

Karate from Okinawa

Okinawa is a cluster of islands to the southwest of the Japan mainland. Up until 1879, Okinawa was an independent kingdom called Ryukyu. People in Ryukyu used powerful kicking, hitting, and striking in battle. This is karate. There are some artifacts from the Kume village that suggest that karate was introduced at a royal celebration in 1867.

Because of its location between China and mainland Japan, Ryukyu had received Chinese emissaries since ancient times (see below).

These visitors brought Chinese science and culture with them, including Chinese martial arts*. It is likely that the people of Ryukyu incorporated this knowledge and expanded on it to create their own style of martial art.

*In Japanese, karate is now written with symbols meaning "empty hand." Originally, it was written as "Chinese hand."

DID YOU KNOW?
What are emissaries?

At one time, the Emperor of China appointed an emissary to each of China's neighboring countries. An emissary is someone who is sent to a foreign country to meet the head of the country.

Emissaries came to Ryukyu twenty-four times from the years 1400 to 1800. One time, a group of several hundred people came with the emissary and stayed for a whole month. The king threw many parties in their honor. Whenever an emissary came, huge banquets were held. It's now thought that it was at one of these banquets where karate was introduced.

Reproduction of a banquet for the diplomats

Defense without weapons

A major reason for the development of karate was that weapons were banned twice for the people of Ryukyu. King Sho Shin banned them in 1526, and they stayed banned for the fifty years of his reign. Weapons were banned again from 1609 onwards, when Ryukyu was invaded by Japan.

The people of Ryukyu still needed a way to defend themselves. They developed ways to fight using their bare hands or common farming tools. People practiced karate in secret while spreading it to every part of Ryukyu.

Over time, karate became so widespread and accepted that in 1901, karate started being taught in schools in the capital city of Shuri.

Below: A scene of elementary school students demonstrating karate. This picture was taken in 1937 in Okinawa.

From Okinawa to Tokyo

The person who is given credit for introducing Okinawan karate to the rest of Japan was Gichin Funakoshi. Funakoshi was a teacher and studied karate on his own. In 1922, he unveiled karate at the first Sports Exhibition sponsored by the Ministry of Education. This was the first time karate had been introduced anywhere outside of Okinawa.

Funakoshi taught the disciples of the founder of judo, Jigoro Kano, everything he knew. After that, four main schools* of karate developed. These were the Shotokan school that came from Funakoshi, the Goju school opened by Chojun Miyagi, the Shito school established by Kenwa Mabuni, and the Wado School started by one of Funakoshi's disciples, Hironori Otsuka. Many other styles of karate have developed from these four main ones.

*"School" as it is used here means one organization that has used the same techniques since its founding.

Karate versus karate-*do*

The suffix -*do* means "way" or "path" in Japanese. Adding it to the name of a martial art suggests that it is more than just a study of how to fight. Judo, kyudo, and kendo were once called jujutsu, kyujutsu and kenjutsu. The name change started with judo.

In 1882, the modern-day "father of judo," Jigoro Kano, started a new movement based on jujutsu. He gave his movement the name of "judo," which focused on respecting others and working for the good of society. Soon other martial arts also started using –*do*. This change in philosophy is seen today in the concept of using martial arts for self-defense rather than for attacking others. However, most people use the term "karate" rather than "karate-*do*."

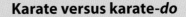

2

Expansion to the Universities

The style of karate introduced by Gichin Funakoshi spread quickly among the universities, and karate clubs were formed. Karate soon became a central part of the universities.

Development around universities

In 1922, Gichin Funakoshi introduced karate at the First Sports Exhibition. He went to Keio University in 1924, and then to Tokyo University in 1926, to start karate clubs. Soon, karate clubs were being created all over Japan.

At the time, many clubs developed their own style because each was independent. To help share knowledge, fourteen schools from Western and Eastern Japan started the All-Japan Student Karate Demonstration Tournament in 1941. This competition drew from universities that were affiliated with any of the four main karate schools: Shotokan, Wado, Goju, and Shito. This first competition greatly influenced the later expansion of karate.

Founding karate clubs created at major universities after 1924

- Balance - Keio University (1924)
- Tokyo Imperial University (1926)
- Toyo University (1927)
- Ritsumeikan University (1929)
- Takushoku University (1930)
- Waseda University (1933)
- Hosei University (1936)
- Tokyo University of Agriculture (1934)
- Meiji University (1936)
- Doshisha University (1937)
- Kyoto Imperial University (1940) (now Kyoto University)

The first university karate club at Keio University. The fourth from the right (in the very front) is Gichin Funakoshi.

The Waseda club at its inception. At the very center is Gichin Funakoshi.

 # War and karate

After 1922, karate was primarily centered at universities, and spread between students. However, when World War II started in 1939, those students were called into the army. This slowed karate's expansion greatly.

In 1945, Japan was defeated and was occupied by the United States Army. The teaching of kendo and judo were banned because the U.S. thought that Japan's fighting spirit was fostered by martial arts.

However, karate was not included in the ban, in part because many clubs had already stopped practicing. Soon new clubs started forming and quickly spread to students all over Japan.

A unifying organization

Before the war, there wasn't much interaction between karate groups from different universities. After the war, this changed. Finally in 1957, the Japan Student Karate Federation was established. This brought together karate organizations and led to the founding of the Japan Karate Federation (JKF) in 1964.

A group photo of the people involved in the first joint demonstration competition after the war in 1950.

DID YOU KNOW?

When did the meaning of "karate" change?

Originally, "karate" was written with characters that meant "Chinese hand." This was because many of its techniques were taken from Chinese martial arts.

This became a problem for Gichin Funakoshi when he wanted to promote karate. Japan was at war with China at the time, and he knew something named "Chinese hand" would be very unpopular. He chose to write "karate" with characters that meant "empty hand," even though the word was pronounced the same way. This would be like writing "legendary feet" instead of "legendary feat." It's pronounced the same way, but changing the spelling changes the meaning. In 1935, Gichin Funakoshi wrote a book called "Karate-do Kyohan." This was the first time "karate" was written with the characters that meant "empty hand."

A 1935 version of
Karate-do Kyohan

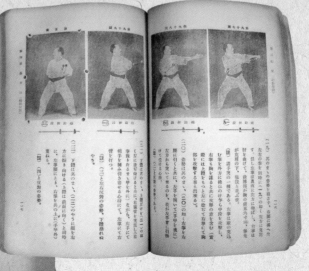

Expansion and Competition

In 1957, the Japan Student Karate Federation was established, and major competitions started.

Kata and *kumite*

From the beginning, karate was centered on the practice and repetition of *kata*, or forms. However, starting in 1922, a one-on-one fighting technique called *kumite*, or sparring, was used. When university students practiced with each other, they did *kumite*.

In 1957, the Japan Student Karate Federation started holding official competitions with the Japan University Karate Championships (see page 18), but during this competition they still did *kumite*. The following year, the Japan Student Karate Tournament was launched.

Basic rule: "No contact"

Karate is a martial art that you do with bare hands. When karate first developed, there was no protective gear. There was a general rule to stop right before hitting opponents to avoid injuring them.

As one-on-one sparring became more common, more safety measures were necessary. One of those safety measures was the 1957 "No Contact" rule. The Japan Karate Federation also used the rule. Although some tournaments allow contact, the no-contact rule is used in tournaments and competitions everywhere.

Materials from the 1957 and 1958 Tournaments

The 1st Japan Student Karate Championships group photograph: pictured are the officials and competitors from various universities.

Protective gear

Although there is a "no contact" rule, protective gear is for those times when contact is made accidentally. In the early days of competition, if a competitor was injured, he had to leave the competition.

Protective gear was first used in 1981 (see page 20). At first, it was just pads for the hands, but the following year, headgear was introduced. Now three safety devices are commonly used: hand pads, protective gear for the face and head, and a body guard to soften blows to the chest. A mouthpiece is often used when headgear is not required.

From open-weight to weight divisions

Originally, competitors were not paired up by size. This open-weight system meant that a very large person could fight a very small one. However, size often equals power. Concern grew that having mismatched competitors fight each other was too dangerous.

In response, a size hierarchy was implemented in the 1981 National Sports Festival, consisting of lightweight, middleweight, and heavyweight divisions.

However, to this day the Japan Karate Championships (see page 18) are open-weight. The World Karate Championships (see page 21) have both open-weight and divided weight competitions.

An open-weight match at the Japan Karate Championships

A 1982 karate publication from Japan describes protective headgear and how it can lower the impact of a blow.

Japan Karate Federation

How are karate organizations and schools in Japan organized?

An organization beyond the schools

When karate first developed, every village had its own style. At the time, karate was named after the place it came from. So a style that came from the village of Tomari would be called "Tomari-te," or "Tomari-style karate."

After karate was brought to Tokyo, even more schools were developed. Four main schools developed out of these original schools (see page 5).

It soon became necessary to unite karate under one organization for the purpose of popularizing it. With this purpose in mind, the Japan Karate Federation was created in 1964. The organization serves as a model for other countries that are trying to promote karate as a sport.

■ JKF's organizational map

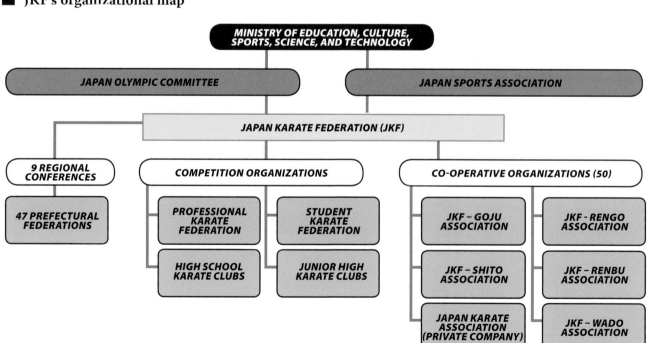

The role of JKF

JKF's purpose is to represent a united Japanese karate. In 1969, the government's Ministry of Education, Culture, Sports, Science, and Technology approved JKF as an organization.

In the same year, the Japan Karate Championships were held for the first time.

Now the JKF has started to sponsor various tournaments. Let's look at the activities below.

■ Tournaments

The Japan Karate Championships are one of many tournaments that are sponsored by, supported by, or put on with the cooperation of the JKF.

The Japan Karate Championships in the Nippon Budokan

■ Accreditation

JKF authorizes the issuing of official *dan*, as well as certificates for umpires and instructors. JKF also holds classes for referee training and trains those who are especially capable for the promotion of karate.

Referee training session

■ Choosing and strengthening a national team

Exceptional competitors are selected for special training. After a period of time training in other *dojo*, an experience known as *gasshuku*, they can represent the national team in international tournaments.

The 2010 World Karate Championship gold medalists and the national team coach

■ Maintenance and improvement of the rules

The World Karate Federation (WKF) plays a central role as it helps develop, maintain, and improve the rules of the sport.

On the left: The Japanese representative at a WKF conference

Karate in schools

Starting in 2012, martial arts classes were required in Japanese middle schools. They are sometimes offered in U.S. schools as well.

Karate in schools

At the beginning of the 20th century, you could take karate classes in Okinawan schools. Because university clubs were available, in-school karate classes were usually just introductory.

However, there may be more opportunities to try karate in school in the future. Starting in 2012, all Japanese junior high students were required to take a martial arts class, boys and girls alike. The schools may offer up to nine* martial arts.

*Including aikido, karate, kyudo, kendo, jukendo, judo, sumo, naginata, and shorinji kempo.

One junior high school's experiment

In 2010, students at Aoyagi Junior High in Japan took a karate class as experiment for the 2012 requirement. This is what they came up with for the benefits of karate in schools:

- **Compared to judo (which needs *tatami* mats) and kendo (which requires a bamboo sword and protective gear), karate requires very little gear or equipment.**
- **Karate is relatively safe because most of the time you are practicing *kata* individually and there is a rule against hitting your opponent.**

Even a simple punch has many details to learn: fist formation, angle of the wrist, stance, rotation of the arm, and mental focus.

What was the first day of class like?

A physical education and a home economics teacher with martial arts experience guided the class.

First, students learned about the importance of courtesy and respect for one's opponent. Then they learned the way of the *rei* (bow) and how to stand. Next they tried punching.

In the class, they learned a basic stance and tried to punch and break the newspapers their friends held. It was the first time many of them had tried martial arts, but the students had fun while being inventive. After class was over, many of the students wrote down their thoughts.

In this school, even after the class is done, the experience will live on in other martial arts classes.

Practicing punching

Punching to break the newspaper. Paper is thin but strong.

Students learn how to sit and bow correctly.

What did the students think?

- This is the first time I learned karate. I came to understand that karate is not mainly about hurting people. It's different from what I thought, so I was surprised.
- Doing *seiza* (a special kneeling stance) hurt.
- It was hard to break the paper with my punch. But it was fun.
- My legs hurt and standing was hard, but it was interesting.
- I knew a little about karate. Today's gym class was very interesting.

13

From Japan to the World

*Karate did not just travel from Okinawa to Japan.
It also has been taught in every corner of the world.*

Pre-World War II global expansion

One example of someone who went abroad to teach karate was Kentsu Yabu, who had the same karate teacher in Okinawa as Gichin Funakoshi. Yabu went to the U.S. at the same time that Funakoshi went to Tokyo, in 1922. In 1934, Chojun Miyagi, the founder of the Gojo School, went to Hawaii to teach karate.

Chojun Miyagi (the 2nd from the right) was invited by a local newspaper to go to Hawaii to spread karate. In the right corner is the owner of the newspaper.

Full-fledged global expansion

Once World War II started it was difficult to spread karate outside of Japan. After the war ended, the United States occupied Japan for several years. While there, the American soldiers requested demonstrations of judo, kendo, and karate. That is when karate-*do* became known as "karate" to non-Japanese.

In 1952, U.S. Air Force physical training officers stayed in Japan to learn karate and other Japanese martial arts. In 1953, at the invitation of the U.S. Air Force, Japanese martial arts teachers went to the American mainland and taught martial arts. Riding this trend, karate started its full-fledged global expansion.

Non-Japanese karate practitioners

Around 1950, those who had trained in university clubs in Japan started traveling abroad to North and South America, Europe, the Philippines, and other Asian countries. Little by little, karate was introduced to every region of the world. Some people opened up local *dojo* to teach karate. Many Japanese who opened *dojo* gave financial support to local people who wanted to open up their own *dojo* – all for the purpose of spreading karate.

These people helped karate to spread all over the world.

Start of international tournaments

As karate took hold in the global community, the demand for competitions grew. In response, the predecessor of the WKF, the World United Karate Organization (WUKO) was created in 1970. That same year, the First World Karate Championships were held in the Nippon Budokan.

The World Karate Championships take place every two years. In 2008, the 19th World Championships took place in Tokyo. A record-breaking 99 countries participated, with close to a thousand competitors. These numbers clearly show the expansion of karate.

A sparring competition at the 1st World Karate Championships in 1970

The 19th World Karate Championships opening ceremony – you can see every nation's flag.

6

International Karate

Let's look at how competitors from different countries prepare for international competitions, at their strengths and successes.

Asia

In world tournaments, Japan almost always wins the most medals. However, other countries' successes are remarkable, especially Iran and Kazakhstan in the male *kumite* competitions. Indonesia, Malaysia, Vietnam and others threaten Japan's position in the female *kumite* competitions.

Japan usually wins the *kata* championships. However, Vietnam's Hoang Ngan Nguyen won the female *kata* championship in the 2008 World Championships in Tokyo.

Africa

There are more than 50 countries on the African continent, but until the 1980s, only Egypt and a few others participated in the world tournaments. In 1990, Egypt, South Africa, Senegal, Tunisia and others joined. It is expected that the number of African countries participating will grow.

Oceania

As of late, the only country from Oceania that has been able to participate at the international level is Australia. Australia has many immigrants, so competitors from Australia are of European, American, Chinese, and Japanese descent.

Also, recently Australia has collaborated with New Zealand's karate practitioners.

Hoang Ngan Nguyen (Vietnam)

Pan-America

Two athletes from Hawaii won World Championship titles in 2002. Since winning, they have become internationally famous. Recently, World Champions have come from Mexico, Chile, Venezuela, Brazil and other nations. Venezuela's athletes have been trained so well that in 2010, they won both the women's and men's *kata* championship.

Europe

European countries are full of highly skilled competitors. Both men and women on Europe's national teams have won World Championship titles many times. It can be said that Europe leads with Japan when it comes to international karate.

Until the 1990s, Britain, France, Spain, Italy, and Turkey were dominant, but as of late Azerbaijan, Serbia, Russia, Hungary, Croatia and others are rapidly becoming more powerful.

World champions

Below are the people who won championship titles in Serbia in 2010. Notice that these champions come from all over the world.

Women's Individual *Kumite*	
Under 50kg	Hong Li – China
Under 55kg	Miki Kobayashi – Japan
Under 61kg	Kristina Mah – Australia
Under 68kg	Yadira Lira – Mexico
Over 68kg	Greta Vitelli – Italy

Men's Individual *Kumite*	
Under 60kg	Douglas Santos Brose – Brazil
Under 67kg	Dimitrios Triantafyllis – Greece
Under 75kg	Rafael Aghayev – Azerbaijan
Under 84kg	Slobodan Bitevic – Serbia
Over 84kg	Dejan Umicevic – Serbia

Women's Team *Kumite*	France
Men's Team *Kumite*	Serbia
Women's Individual *Kata*	Yohanna Sanchez – Venezuela
Men's Individual *Kata*	Antonio Diaz – Venezuela
Women's Team *Kata*	Japan
Men's Team *Kata*	Italy

The 2010 20th World Cup Men's Team *Kumite* medalists

Japanese Tournaments

Because karate originated in Japan, winning a karate tournament in Japan is a great accomplishment. There are many tournaments. Let's look at the ones that decide the nation's best.

Fight to be Japan's best!

▶ Japan Karate Championships

This tournament has a long history. The first competition was held in 1969 at the Nippon Budo-kan. The most recent was the 38th Championship in 2010. One team for each age group from each prefecture* of Japan competes to be the nation's best. There are also individual competitions and open weight *kumite* competitions.

*A prefecture is roughly equivalent to an American state.

▶ Japan University Karate Championships

There are two tournaments to decide the university championship, but this one is for the team championship. The first one took place in 1957 with 32 university karate clubs participating.

▶ Japan Student Karate Championships

This decides the individual student champions. The first one was held in 1958. There were 15 competitors representing East and West Japan. It was originally called the East-West Match.

The men's team *kumite* competition at the Japan Karate Championships

Japan Karate Championships: A large audience always gathers to see who will be the champions of Japan.

The men's *kumite* team is made up of five people. Each women's *kumite* team is made up of three people.

Japan's best high school, junior high and elementary school athletes

In the U.S., junior high and high schools typically compete against each other in sports such as swimming, wrestling, and track. Athletes represent their school but compete individually, and division champions go on to compete at the regional and state level. In Japan, karate competitions are held in a similar way. One difference is that even elementary schools have karate competitions!

▶ Inter-High School Karate Championships

Any school that did well in primary competitions can participate in this competition. Participants can be from 10th – 12th grade, but each school is only allowed two individual competitors and one team.

▶ National High School Karate Contest

Along with Inter-High, this competition decides the high school champions. This competition is for 10th and 11th grade and any team can compete.

▶ Junior High Karate Championships

Four teams and four individuals compete. These teams and individuals qualify during preliminary competitions.

▶ National Junior High Karate Contest

Seventh and eighth graders compete to determine the champions for individual *kata* and *kumite*.

▶ National Boys and Girls Karate Championships

This competition in individual *kumite* and *kata* is held for students in grades 1-6. Two people from every prefecture participate. Whoever had the highest points in preliminary competitions can participate.

The 2010 Junior High Karate Championships' men's team competition

A demonstration during the opening ceremony of the 2010 Inter-High Championships

Competing for the *kata* championship title at the National Boys and Girls Karate Championships

平成22年度 全国 高等学校 総合体育大会
第37回 全国 高等学校 空手道選手権大会

Other tournaments

▶ National Sports Festival

The National Sports Festival is Japan's biggest sports festival, and its purpose is to expand sports and improve the nation's strength. Karate has been included since the 36th Festival in 1981. The male best overall score wins the Emperor's trophy; the female best overall score wins the Empress Trophy.

● Men and women's adult *kumite* competition (individual, by weight divisions)

● Co-ed team competition

● children's team and individual's *kumite* competition

▶ National Children's Martial Arts Training Tournament

This is for elementary and junior high students and happens once a year in the Nippon Budo-kan. Students train for one day and then compete. There is no ranking, only prizes for excellence and effort. Besides karate, eight other martial arts are offered such as aikido, kendo, and judo.

● Boys' and girls' basic training

● Competition training (team *kumite* and *kata*)

▶ Japan Sports Masters

This is for those who have trained in a sport for nearly their entire lives and are masters of their sport. Since 2001, karate has been included. All male participants are over 40 and female participants are over 35, and they have competed with many different clubs.

The 2010 National Sports Festival in Chiba: Men's heavyweight kumite competition

Men and women's individual *kumite* and *kata* competitions

International Tournaments

Karate has spread throughout the entire world, and outstanding karate practitioners can be found everywhere. Let's look at those tournaments that attract the strongest competitors.

Fight to be the world's best!

▶ World Karate Championships

The World Karate Federation (WKF) sponsors this competition. It has been held every two years since 1970. In 2010, about 1100 competitors from 88 nations and regions came to compete. Individual *kumite* competitions are divided into weight classes (see page 23), but in 2010 there were also open-weight competitions. During this tournament, JKF offers seminars and the WKF certifies referees.

Women's *kumite* match

The Japan Women's team showed determination during the *kata* competition.

▶ World Games

Often called the "Second Olympics," the World Games are for sports that aren't included in the Olympics. The International Olympic Committee (IOC) doesn't allow the competition to happen the same year as the Olympics, so it happens a year after the summer Olympics. Karate has been a part of the World Games since the first one was held in 1981. The competition is similar to the World Karate Championships, but it is individual competition only with both open-weight and weight classifications.

▶ Sport Accord World Combat Games

This tournament started in 2010. It is a competition including martial arts from Japan (karate, judo, kendo, sumo, aikido, etc.), Thailand (muay thai), Russia (sambo), and China (kung fu). Men and women compete in individual sparring. The first year, there were 13 competitions; close to 1600 people participated from 60 countries and regions. Like the Olympics, it takes place every four years.

▶ Fight to be Asia's best!

▶ Asian Karate Championships

Karate's homeland is Japan, which is part of Asia. Recently China, Vietnam, Iran, and other Asian nations have also become very powerful and are some of the leading countries. This tournament happens every two years to determine who is best in Asia.

▶ Asian Games

This happens every four years and takes place two years after the Olympics; it is called the "Asian Olympics." JKF has lobbied the IOC for karate to become an Olympic sport, so far unsuccessfully. However, in 1994, Hiroshima, Japan hosted the Asian Games (see page 24-25). In 2010, at the 16th summer games, karate was included as one of the 42 sports.

The women's *kata* medalists at the 2010 Asian Games. Second from the left is the champion from Japan, Rika Usami.

Rika Usami's demonstration

Under-21 international tournaments

▶ Cadet, Junior, and Under-21 World Championships

The Cadet (14–15 years old) and Junior (16–17 years old) Championships attract the strongest practitioners. These competitions were originally held with the Karate World Cup every two years. Starting in 1999, they were held as the Junior and Cadet Championships. The Under-21 Competition was first held in 2011. These tournaments attract competitors from the World Karate Championships, the Senior Championship, and others.

● Cadet and Junior: Men's and women's team and individual *kata*, individual *kumite*

● Under-21: Men's and women's individual *kumite*

▶ Asian Cadet, Junior, and Under-21 World Championships

In 2010, the Under-21 Championship was created to join the Asian Cadet and Junior Championships.

● Cadet and Junior: Men's and women's team and individual *kata*; individual *kumite*

● Under-21: Men's and women's individual *kumite*

Differences according to age

There are many competitions to see who is the best in the world at karate. Your age determines which of the competitions listed below you can enter.

Kumite competitions are divided by the weight classes shown below. Remember, the World Karate Championship also has open-weight competitions.

Tournament divisions according to age	
Cadet Championship	14–15 years old
Junior Championship	16–17 years old
Under-21 Championship	18–20*
Senior Championship	Over 16 for *kata*, over 18 for *kumite*

* If you are 21, you can participate, but if you have participated in the Senior Championship, you cannot participate in the Under-21 Championship.

Men's weight classes (2010) in kg*	
Cadet	-52, -57, -63, -70, +70
Junior	-55, - 61, -68, -76, +76
Under-21	-68, -78, +78
Senior	-60, -67, -75, -84, +84, Open-weight

* (-) means under; (+) means over

Women's weight classes (2010) in kg*	
Cadet	-47, -54, +54
Junior	-48, -53, -59, +59
Under-21	-53, -60, +60
Senior	-50, -55, -61, -68, +68, Open-weight

* (-) means under; (+) means over

Kumite matches during the Junior and Cadet Championships

Aiming for the Olympics

Recently, efforts have increased around the world to make karate an Olympic sport.

First steps toward the Olympics

As karate has become popular in every part of the globe, the movement calling for karate to become an Olympic sport has become stronger.

Progress was made when it was decided that the 1994 Asian Games (see page 22) would be held in Hiroshima with karate as one of the sports.

In many ways, the Asian Games are the Asian Olympics. In fact, the Olympic Council of Asia, which is a part of the International Olympic Committee (IOC), sponsors the Asian Games. Including karate in the Asian Games was a step on the way to allowing karate as part of the Olympics.

In 1999, the WKF became an official organization of the IOC. Becoming an official organization of the IOC was a very important step. With this, the voice calling for karate to be an Olympic sport has only grown stronger. However, as of 2012, karate had not been approved as an Olympic sport.

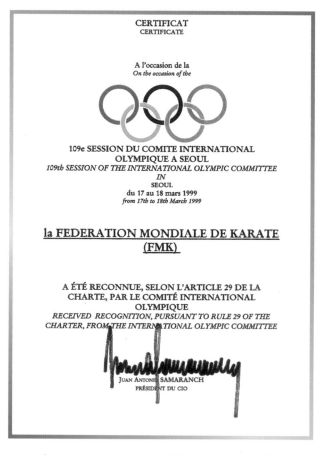

A certificate the IOC sent to the WKF. It certifies the WKF as an official organization of the IOC. The signature on the bottom is of the President of the IOC at the time, Juan Antonio Samaranch.

How the IOC selects Olympic sports

For the IOC to certify events or sports, they must meet the conditions on the right. However, even if conditions are met, it doesn't mean that the event or competition will be certified.

The events and competitions that made up the 2012 Olympics were already chosen at the 2005 IOC conference. While karate was one of five candidates, it was not chosen.

However, the WKF will continue to advocate the adoption of karate as an Olympic sport.

As long as there are children who diligently study karate, there is a chance that some day karate will have its time on the Olympic stage.

Conditions for certification

① For an event to be included in the Summer Olympics, men from at least 75 countries on four continents and women from 40 countries on three continents must regularly compete. In the case of the Winter Olympics, participants from 25 countries on 3 continents must regularly compete.

② The sport or event must be recognized internationally. Also, a World or Continental Championship must have been held more than twice.

Competitors from all over the world at an under-21 tournament. If karate becomes an Olympic sport, these athletes will have a new goal to achieve.

Famous people from karate history

There have been many karate practitioners, but let's take a look at some famous Japanese and international karate champions.

Japan

Tsuguo Sakumoto — THREE CONSECUTIVE WORLD CHAMPIONSHIPS

EVENT: MEN'S *KATA*

Born on December 13, 1947 in Okinawa, Japan, Sakumoto graduated from Nippon Sports Science University. Starting in 1984, he accomplished the incredible feat of winning both the Asia Pacific Karate Championships and World Karate Championships three years in a row. He also won the World Cup and World Games two years in a row. He retired from the forefront of karate to become the Japan national team's coach and develop future generations. In April 2003, he became a professor at Okinawa University of Arts. In June 2010, he became the university's 6th president. He is a JKF-certified 8th dan.

Mie Nakayama — THREE CONSECUTIVE WORLD CHAMPIONSHIPS

EVENT: WOMEN'S *KATA*

Nakayama was born on June 18, 1957 in Hyogo Prefecture, Japan. She debuted on the National Team in 1980. In 1982 she won a championship title at the World Karate Championships and went on to win three in all. After retiring from competition, she was Japan's national team coach until 2008.

Yasumasa Shimizu — WORLD CHAMPION

EVENT: MEN'S ABOVE 80kg *KUMITE* AND OTHERS

Shimizu was born on February 24, 1965 in Tokyo, Japan. He graduated from Setagaya Gakuen High School and Nihon University. He participated in the World Karate Championships seven times before he won a gold medal at the World Karate Championships in 1996. He has won four medals in all: two gold and two silver. He has also won four titles from the Japan Karate Championships and five titles from the National Sports Festival. He was a member of the national team for 18 years. In 2010 he became the supervisor for Nihon University's karate club.

Yuki Mimura

EVENT: WOMEN'S *KATA*

Mimura was born on April 5, 1970 in Nagano Prefecture in Japan. She has been practicing karate since second grade. In 1988, at the 9th World Karate Championships, she became the Women's *Kata* Champion at age 18. She proceeded to win championship titles at the 10th, 11th, and 13th World Championships. She also won three consecutive gold medals at the Fukuoka World Women's Cup, a gold medal at the Tokyo International Ladies' Cup, and others. With her activities abroad and at home, she has helped build an era of women athletes.

Atsuko Wakai

EVENT: WOMEN'S *KATA*

Born on September 12, 1971 in Gifu, Japan, she graduated from Kinki University Junior College. She won four consecutive titles at the World Karate Championships, three consecutive titles at the World Games, and four consecutive titles at the Asian Karate Championship. She also won eight consecutive titles at the Japan Karate Championships and five titles at the National Sports Festival. As of 2010, she was the supervisor of the Seino Transportation Company Karate Club.

Tomoko Araga

EVENT: WOMEN'S *KUMITE* UNDER 53kg

Born on February 1, 1985 in Kyoto, Japan, Araga graduated from Kacho Girls High School. While attending Kyoto Sangyo University she became World Karate Champion in 2004 and again in 2006. At the World Karate Championships in 2006, she was also on the team that won gold for Women's Team *Kumite*.

Shinji Nagaki

EVENT: EVENTS: MALE *KUMITE* UNDER 70kg

Nagaki was born on August 4, 1982 in Ehime, Japan. He started practicing karate at age five in his father's *dojo* and went on to study at Okayama Sanyo High School, which is renowned for karate. He graduated from Teikyou University. He won a gold medal during the World Karate Championships in 2004 and again in 2010.

World

Alexandre Biamonti
NINE CONSECUTIVE EUROPEAN CHAMPIONSHIPS

EVENT: MEN'S *KUMITE* UNDER 65kg

Biamanti was born on November 30, 1973 in Marseille, France. After winning nine consecutive European championship titles, Biamonti became known as one of the world's top competitors. Biamonti holds the record for number of consecutive European titles. He also has championship titles from the World Karate Championships in 1998, Europe Championships, Open de Paris, and many other international tournaments.

George Kotaka

EVENT: MEN'S *KUMITE* UNDER 65kg

Kotaka was born on July 28, 1977 in Hawaii. He started practicing karate under his father, Chuzo Kotaka, at age three. He received the first gold medal for the U.S. in 20 years at the 16th World Karate Championships. He also won a championship title at the 19th World Championships. He now teaches at five *dojo* on the island of Oahu and travels around the world conducting seminars.

Elisa Au

EVENT: WOMEN'S *KUMITE* OVER 60kg

Au was born on May 29, 1981 in Honolulu, Hawaii. She started studying at age five under Chuzo Kotaka, the father of George Kotaka (see upper right). She won a gold medal at the World Karate Championships in 2002, and in 2004 won gold medals in both over 60kg and open-weight *kumite*. She graduated from the University of Hawaii with a degree in civil engineering and is lead instructor in her *dojo* in Chicago, Illinois.

Rafael Aghayev

EVENT: MEN'S *KUMITE* UNDER 70/UNDER 75kg

Aghayev was born on March 4, 1985 in Sumgayit, Azerbaijan. The son of a professional soccer player, he started studying karate when he was seven years old. He has won four world championships and seven European championships. He continues to compete worldwide and is a top-ranked competitor.

On the right is Aghayev.

Let's take a look at how karate has grown from its Okinawan origins to take root throughout the world.

Year	Accomplishments
Early 1900s	Karate Is taught in junior high schools in Shuri, Ryukyu (Okinawa).
1922	Gichin Funakoshi demonstrates karate at the 1st Sports Exhibition in Tokyo.
1924	Keio University forms the first ever university karate club.
1926	Tokyo Imperial University (now Tokyo University) forms its karate club.
1935	Gichin Funakoshi changes the spelling of karate in his book *Karate-do Kyohan*.
1941	Japan Student Karate Demonstration Tournament is held.
1945	World War II ends. United States Army bans martial arts.
1957	Establishment of the Japan Student Karate Federation. The 1st Japan University Karate Championships are held.
1958	Japan Student Championships are held.
1964	The Japan Karate Federation (JKF) is established.
1965	Precursor to a global organization, the European Karate Union (EKU) is founded.
1969	The Ministry of Education, Culture, Sports, Science, and Technology officially approves the JKF. The first Japan Karate Championships are held.
1970	World Karate Federation (WKF)'s predecessor, World Union Karate Organization (WUKO) is established. First World Karate Championships are held at the Nippon Budokan.
1981	The 36th National Sports Festival is held. Karate debuts as an official sport. First World Games are held with karate as an official sport.
1985	The International Olympics Committee (IOC) officially recognizes WUKO.
1993	WUKO changes its name to World Karate Federation (WKF).
1994	The 12th Asian Games are held in Hiroshima. Karate is allowed as an official sport.
1999	The IOC officially recognizes the WKF. The 1st Junior and Cadet Championships are held.
2001	The 1st Japan Sports Masters includes karate as an official sport.
2008	The 19th World Karate Championships are held in the Nippon Budokan again.
2010	The 1st Sport Accord World Combat Games are held in Beijing, with karate as an official sport.

1st Sport Accord World Combat Games

INDEX

GLOSSARY

Japanese Translitcration	Pronunciation	Meaning
Budo	*Boo-doe*	Martial Arts
Dan	*Dahn*	Grade or rank
Gasshuku	*Gah-shoo-koo*	Studying at another *dojo*
Goju	*Go-joo*	Goju School
Karate-do	*Kah-rah-teh-doe*	Way of Karate
Karate-do Kyohan	*Kah-rah-teh-doe Kyo-hahn*	The master text of Shotokan karate
Kata	*Kah-tah*	Forms
Kenjutsu	*Ken-joo-tsoo*	Japanese swordmanship
Kumite	*Koo-mee-teh*	Sparring
Kyudo	*Kyoo-doe*	Japanese archery
Kyujutsu	*Kyoo-joo-tsoo*	Way of the bow
Rei	*Ray*	Bow(ing)
Seiza	*Say-za*	Kneel(ing)
Shito	*She-toe*	Shotokan School
Shotokan	*Show-toe-kahn*	Shotokan School
Tatami	*Tah-tah-me*	Traditional Japanese floormat
Tomari-te	*Toh-mah-ree-teh*	Tomari style
Wado	*Wah-doe*	Wado School

WEBSITES

Karate World:
http://www.karatedo.co.jp/index3.htm

World Karate Federation:
http://www.wkf.net/index.php

Japan Karatedo Federation:
http://www.karatedo.co.jp/jkf/jkf-eng/e_index.htm

This edition published in 2013 by The Oliver Press, Inc.
Charlotte Square
5707 West 36th Street
Minneapolis, MN 55416-2510

KARATE MADE SIMPLE: KARATE ORIGINS AND EXPANSION

Original Japanese title: KIHON WO KIWAMERU! KARATEDO: REKISHI TO HATTEN
(Mastering the Basics! Karatedo: History and Development)
© Champ Co., Ltd., 2011
All rights reserved.
Original Japanese edition published in 2011 by Champ Co., Ltd.
English translation rights with Imajinsha Co., Ltd. through Japan UNI Agency, Inc., Tokyo

Library of Congress Cataloging-in-Publication Data

Nakashima, Maiko.
Karate made simple 4 : Karate origins and expansion / Maiko Nakashima with the Japan Karate Federation.
    p. cm. -- (Karate made simple)
Includes bibliographical references and index.
ISBN 978-1-934545-16-4
1. Karate--Juvenile literature. I. Title.
GV1114.3.N363 2012
796.815'3--dc23
                            2012033031

Text: Maiko Nakashima with the Japan Karate Federation
Translation: Chiaki Hasegawa and Goldie Gibbs
U.S. editing: April Stern
U.S. production: Clay Schotzko

Picture Credits:
All images courtesy of Champ Co., Ltd. and Imajinsha Co., Ltd.

ISBN: 978-1-934545-16-4
Printed in the United States of America
17 16 15 14 13   8 7 6 5 4 3 2 1